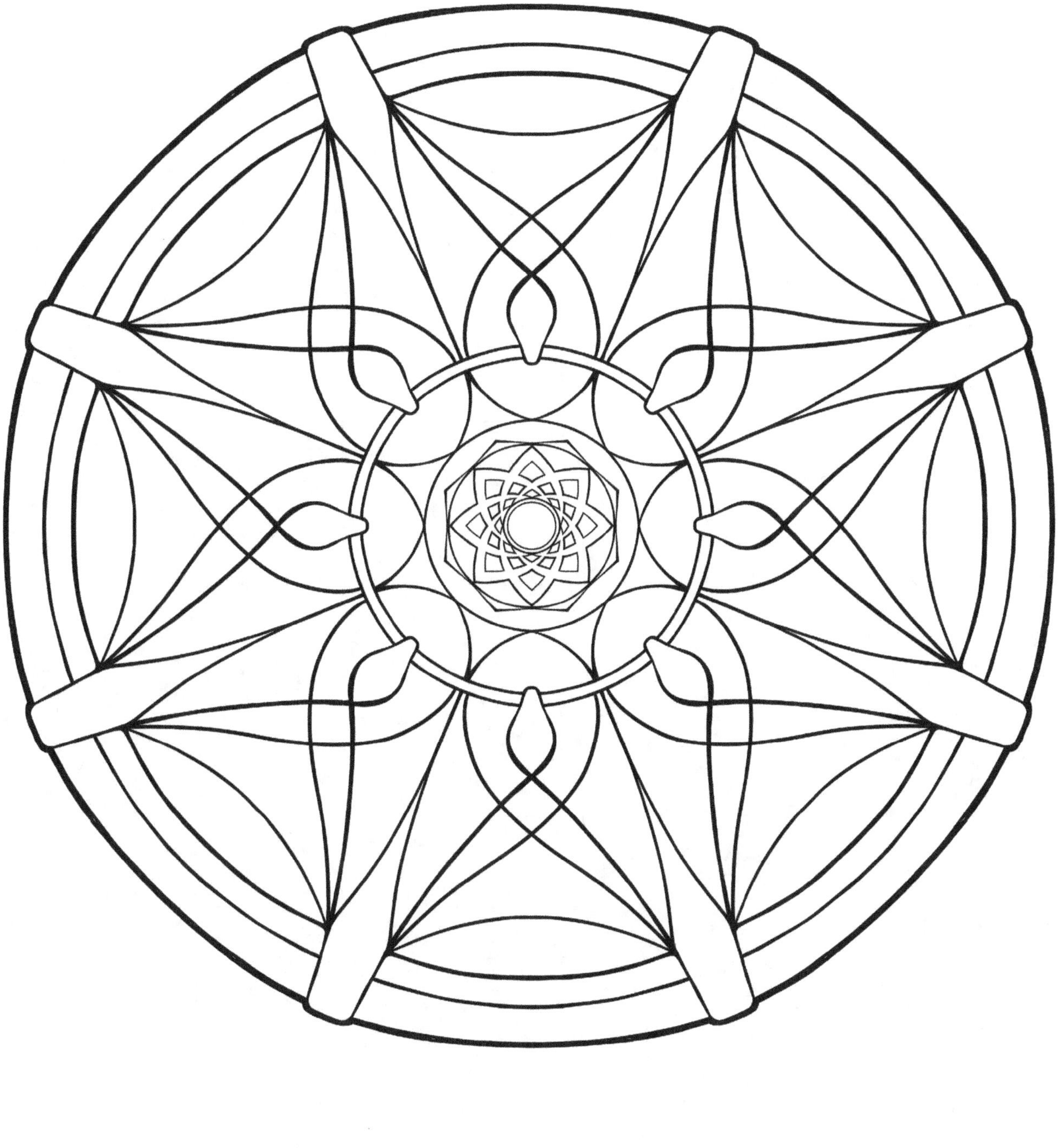

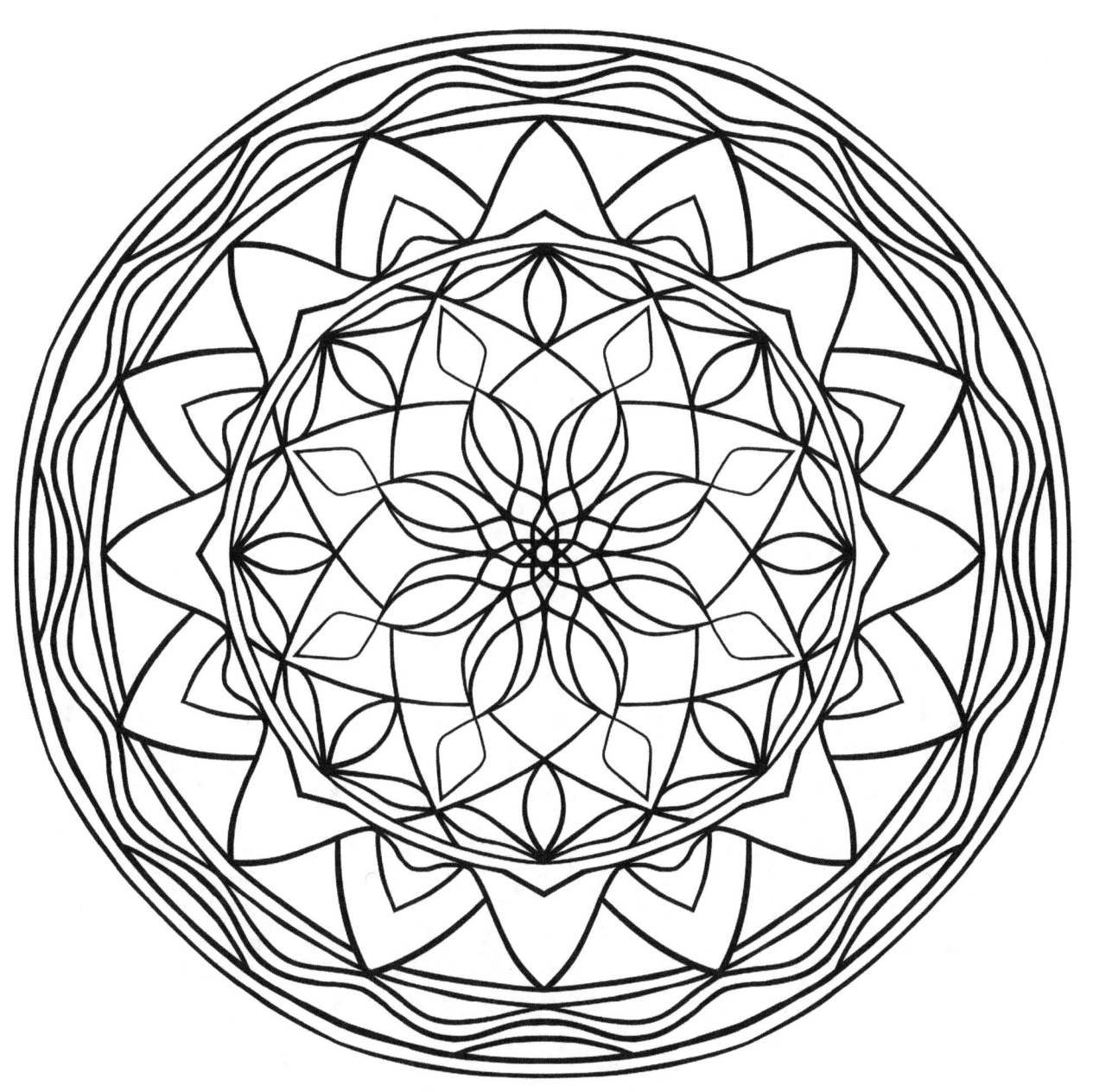

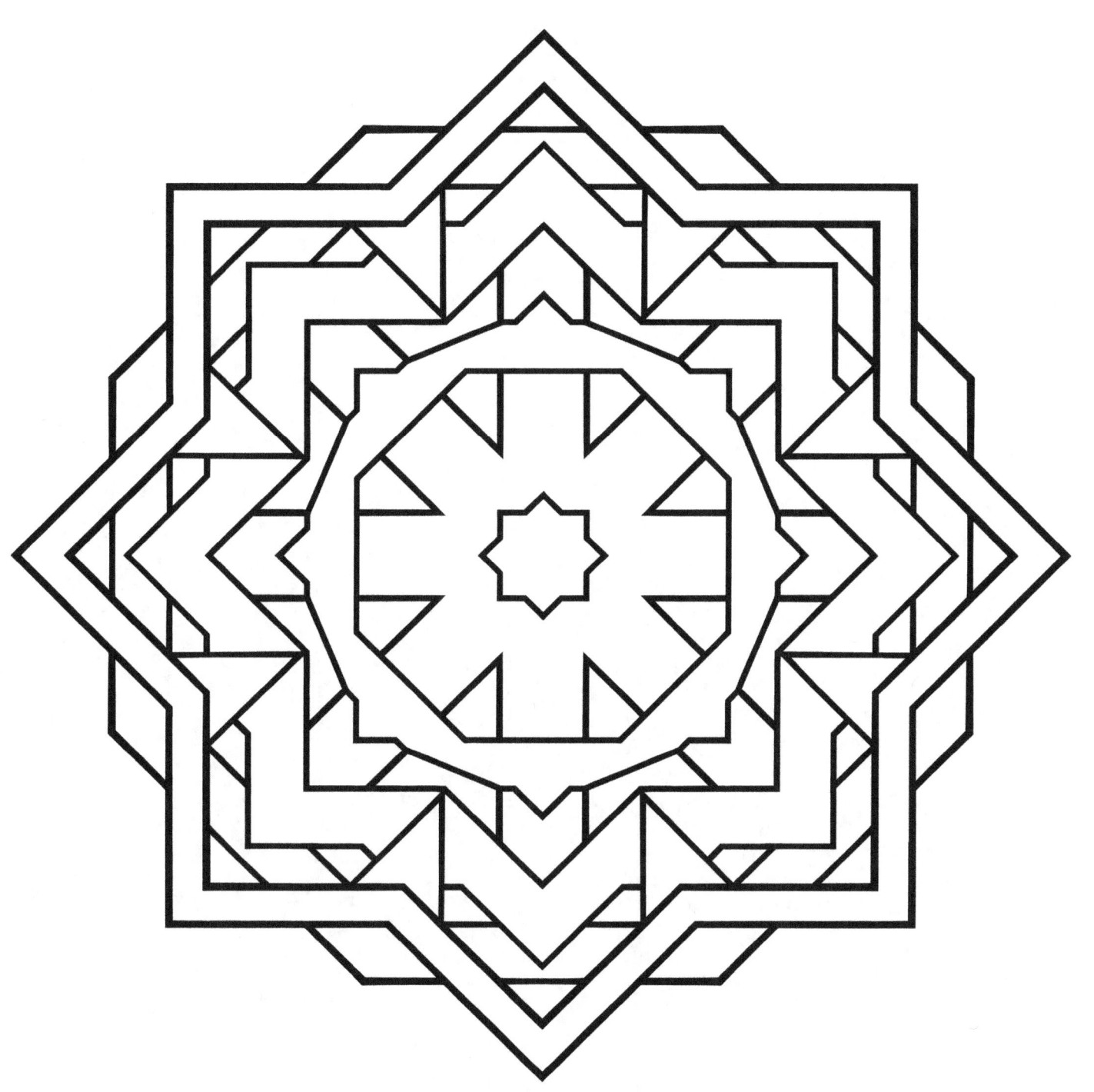

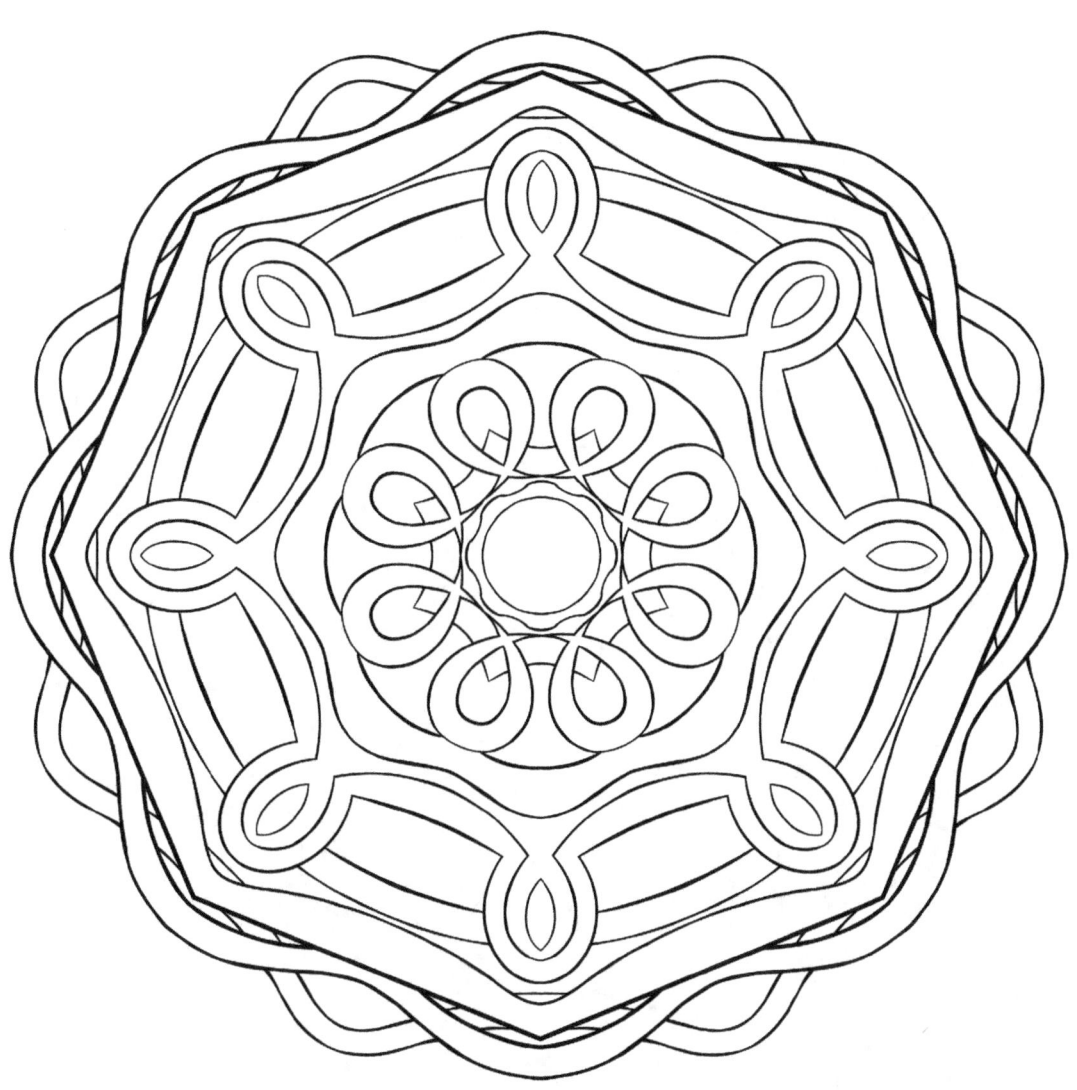

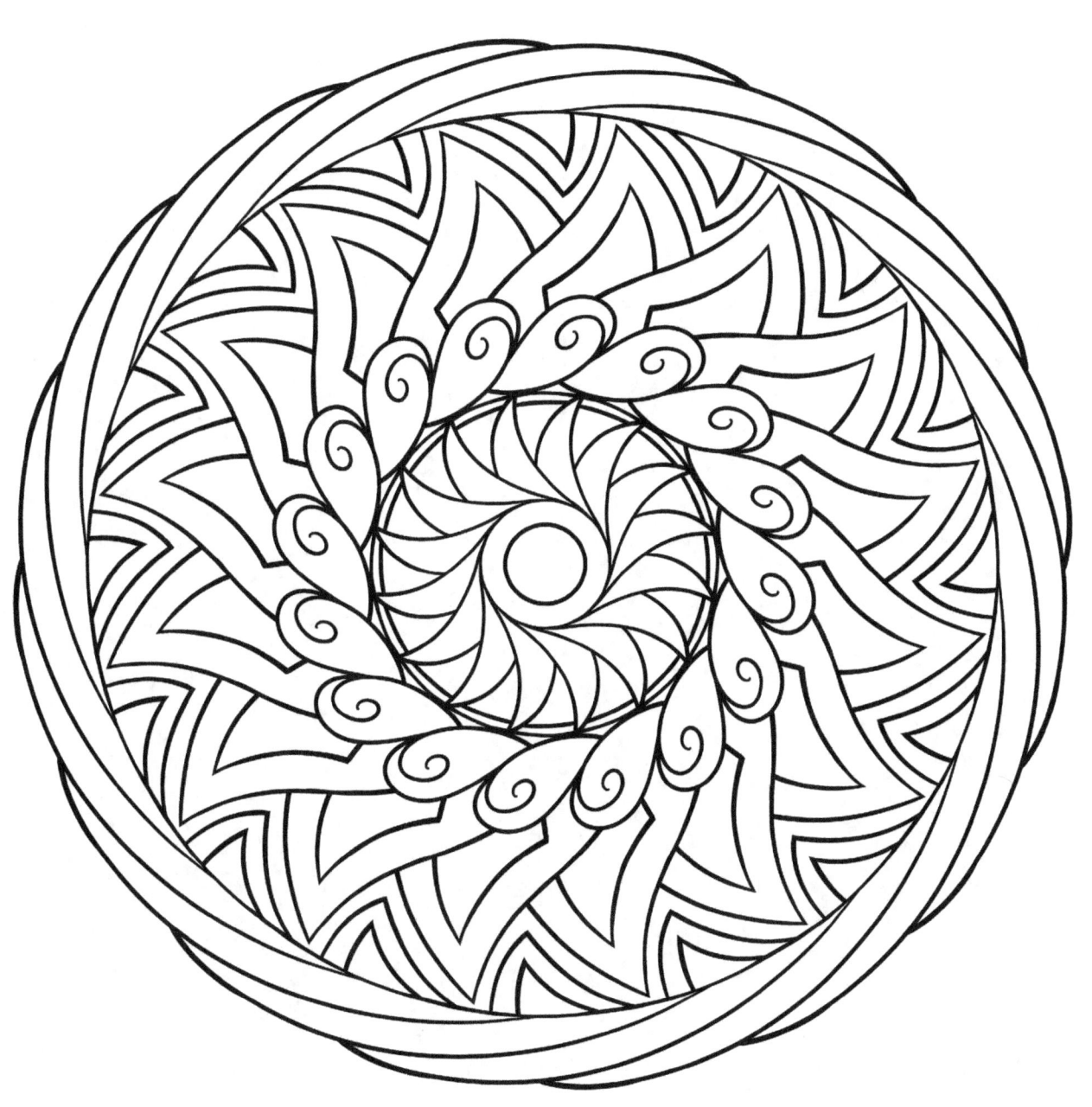

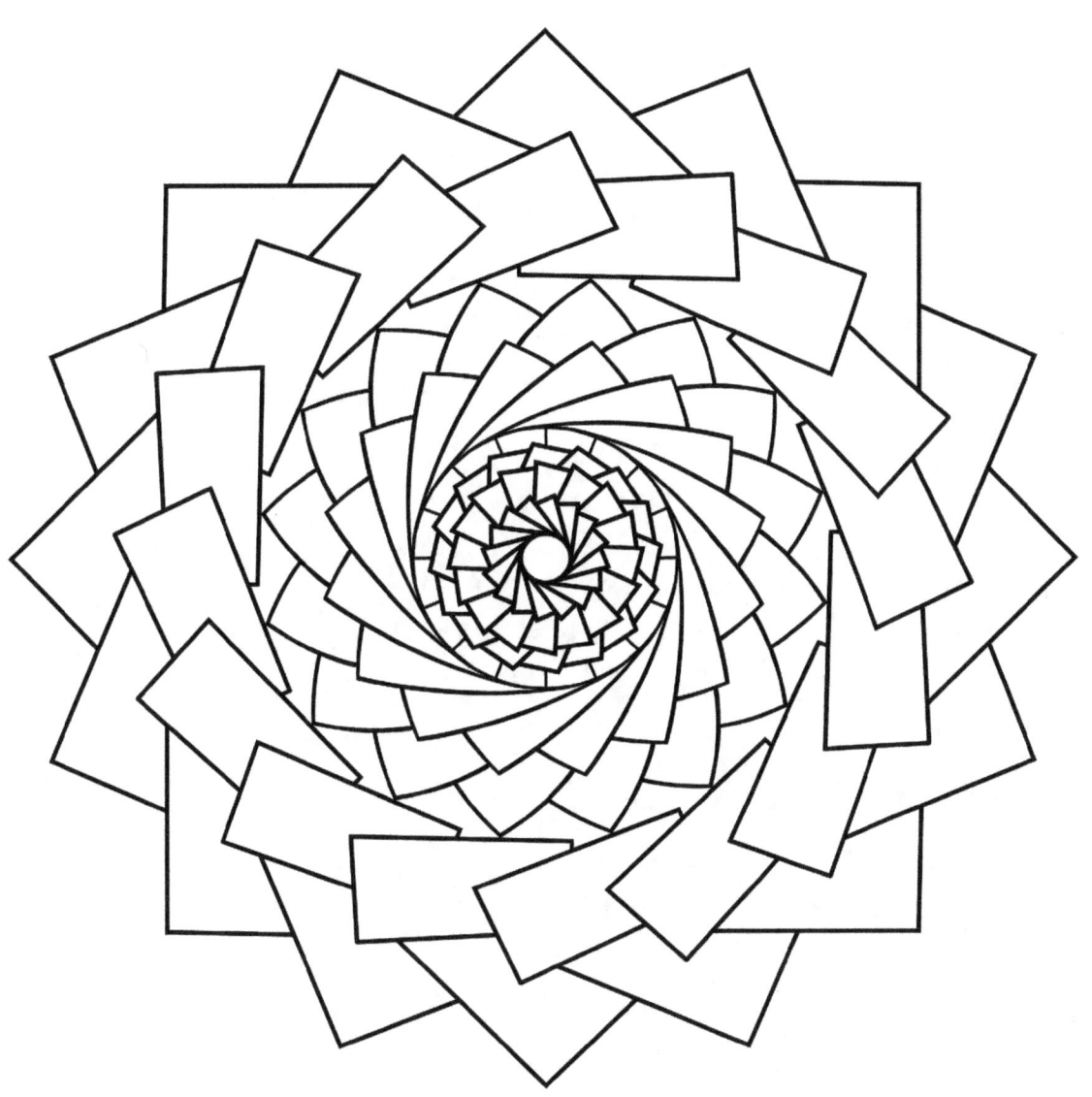

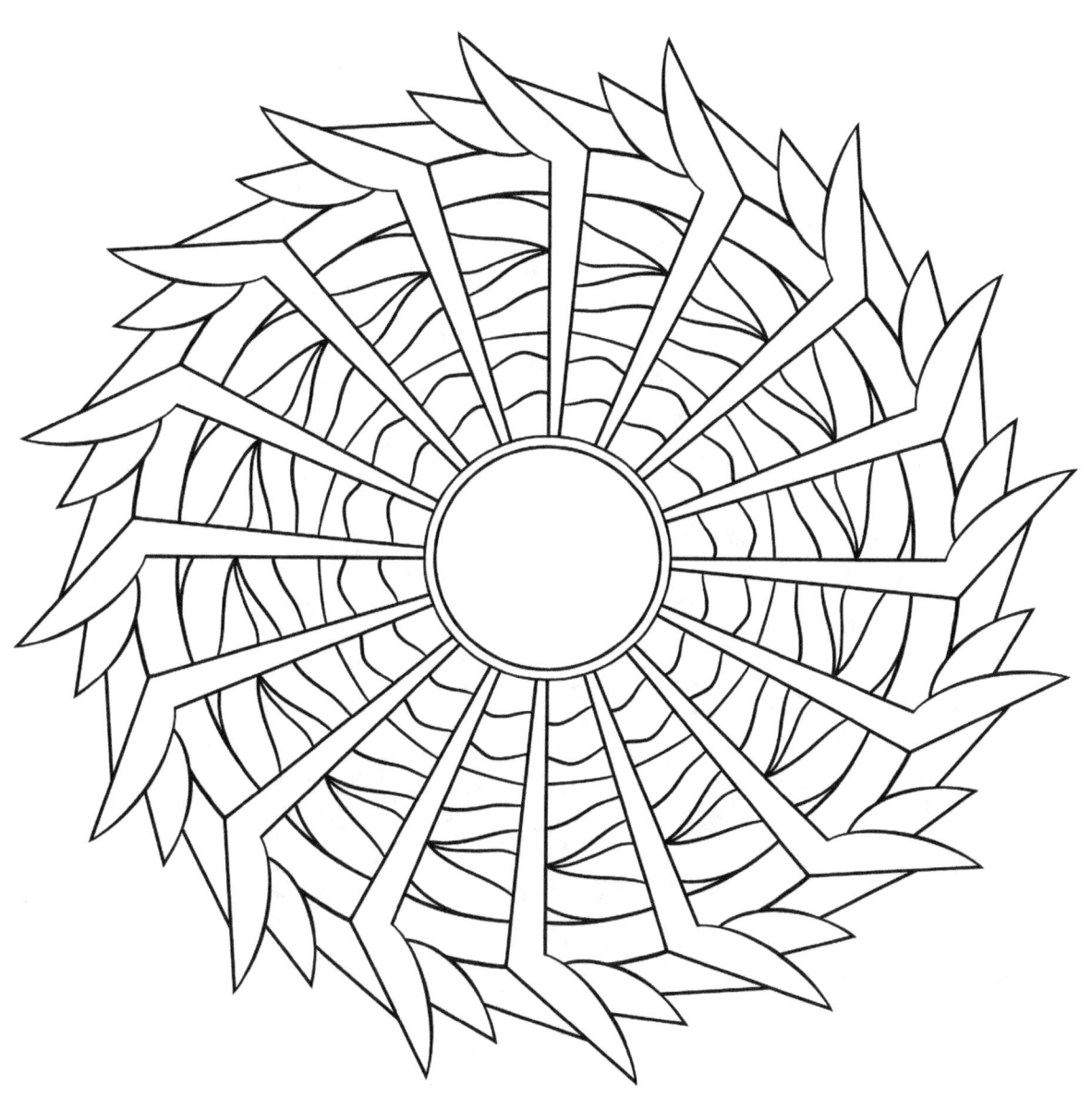

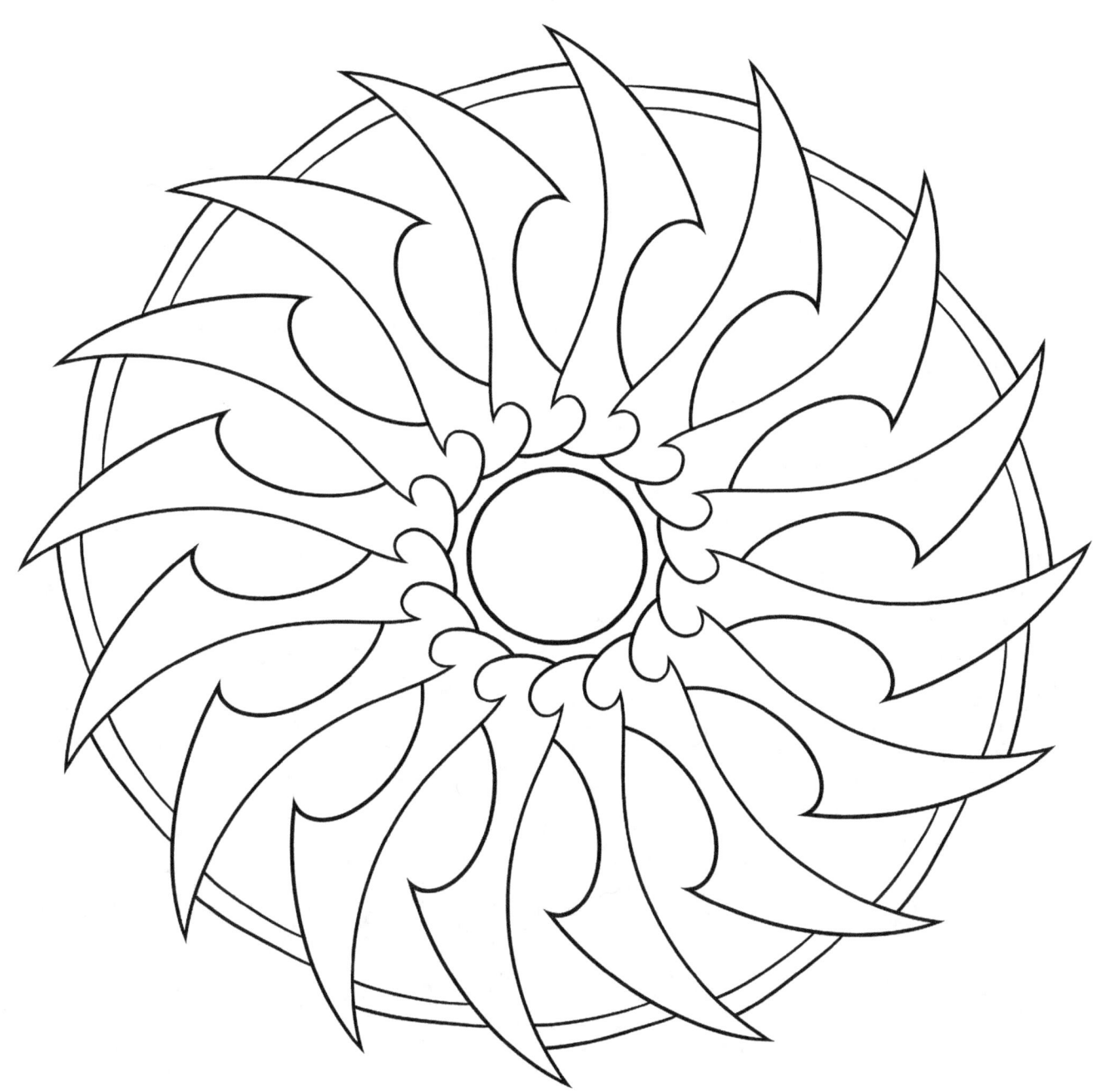

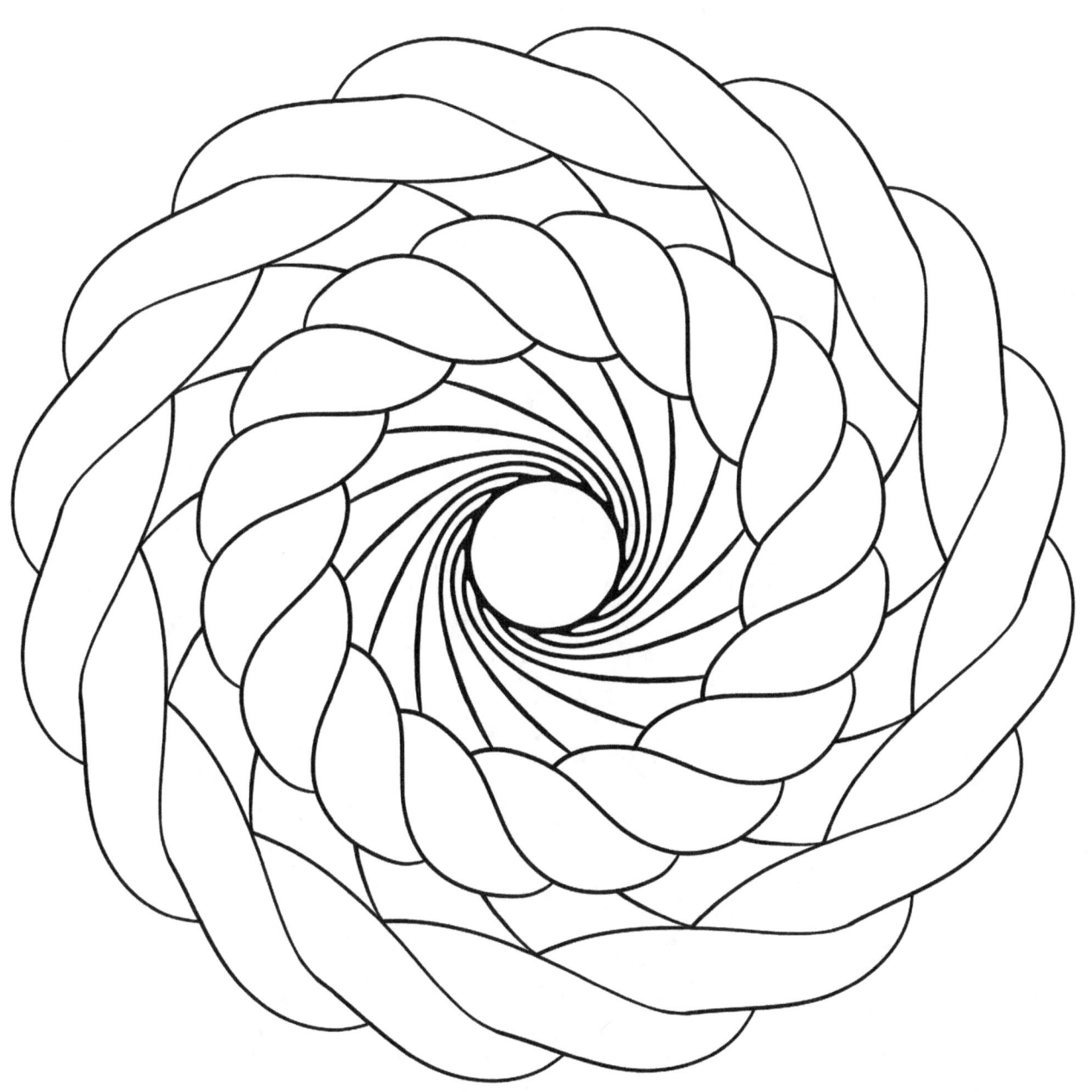

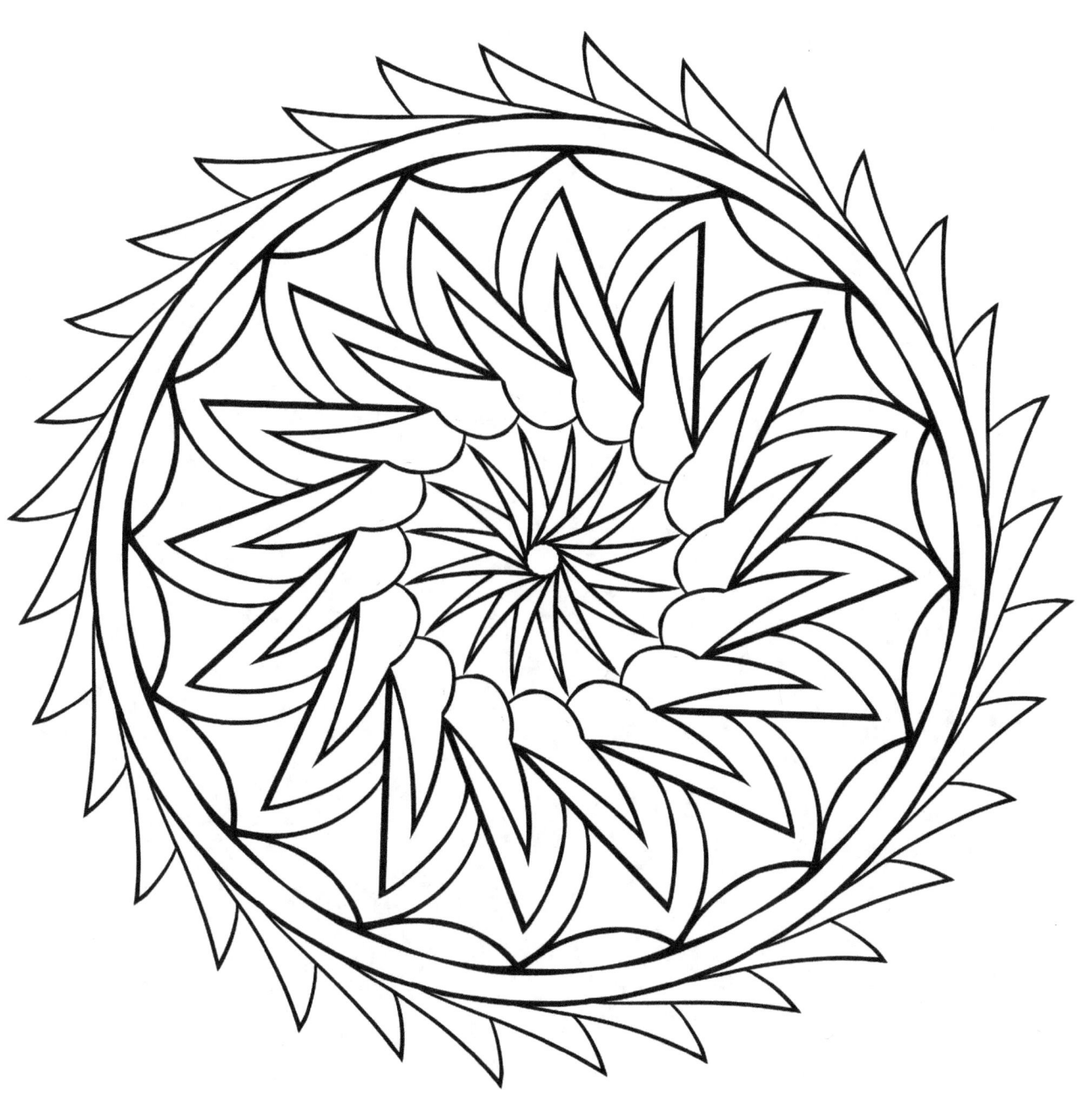

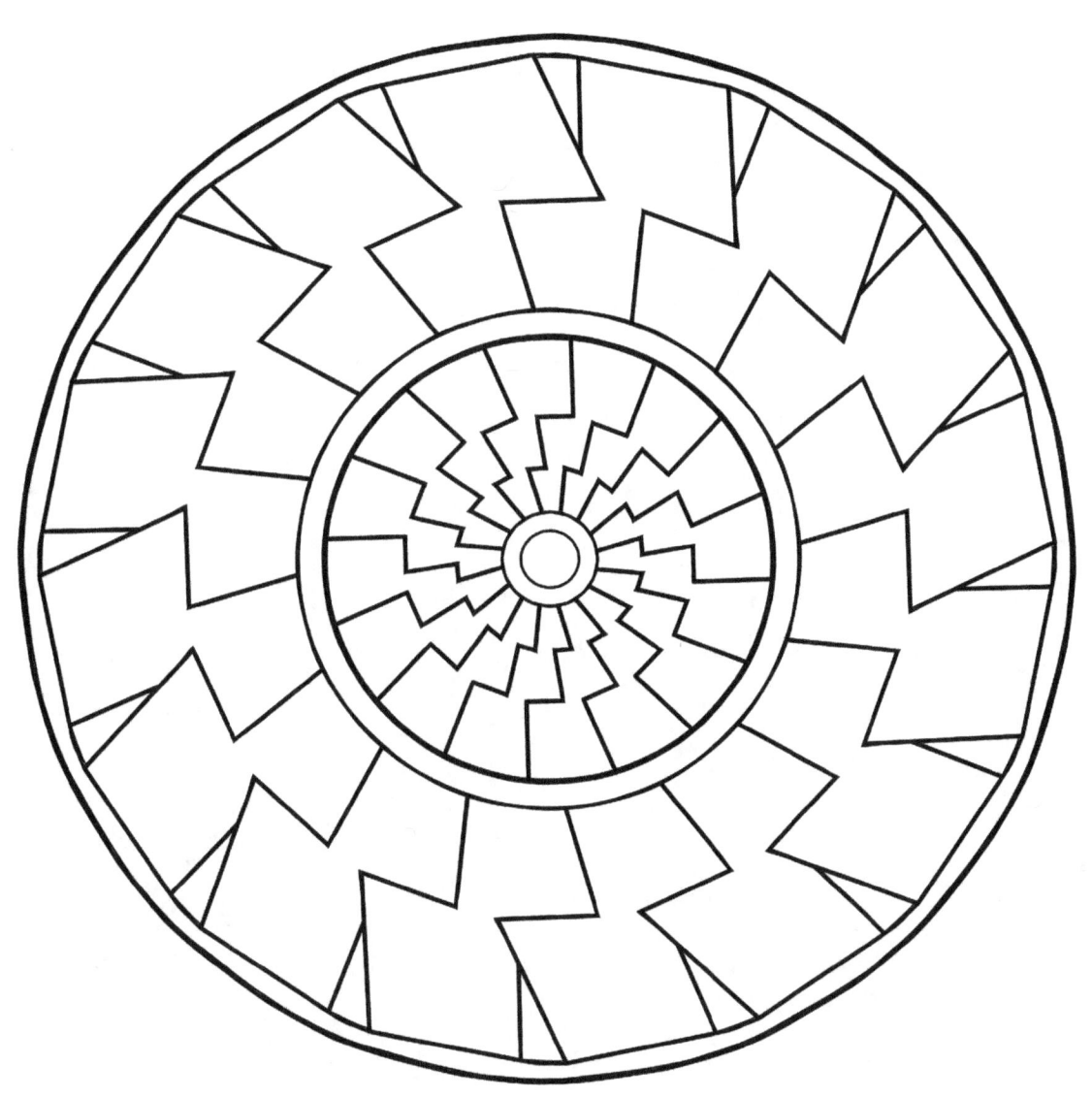

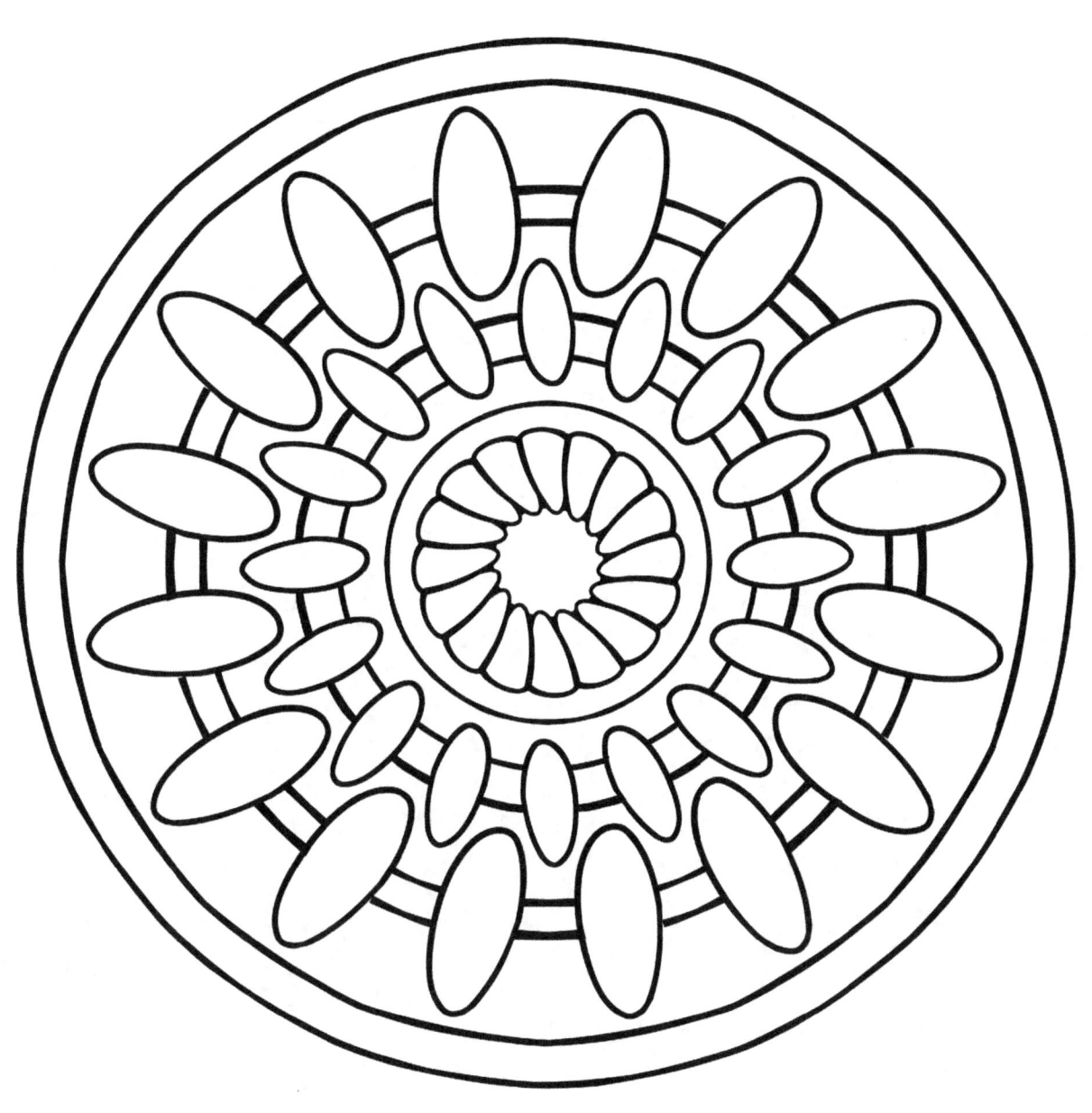

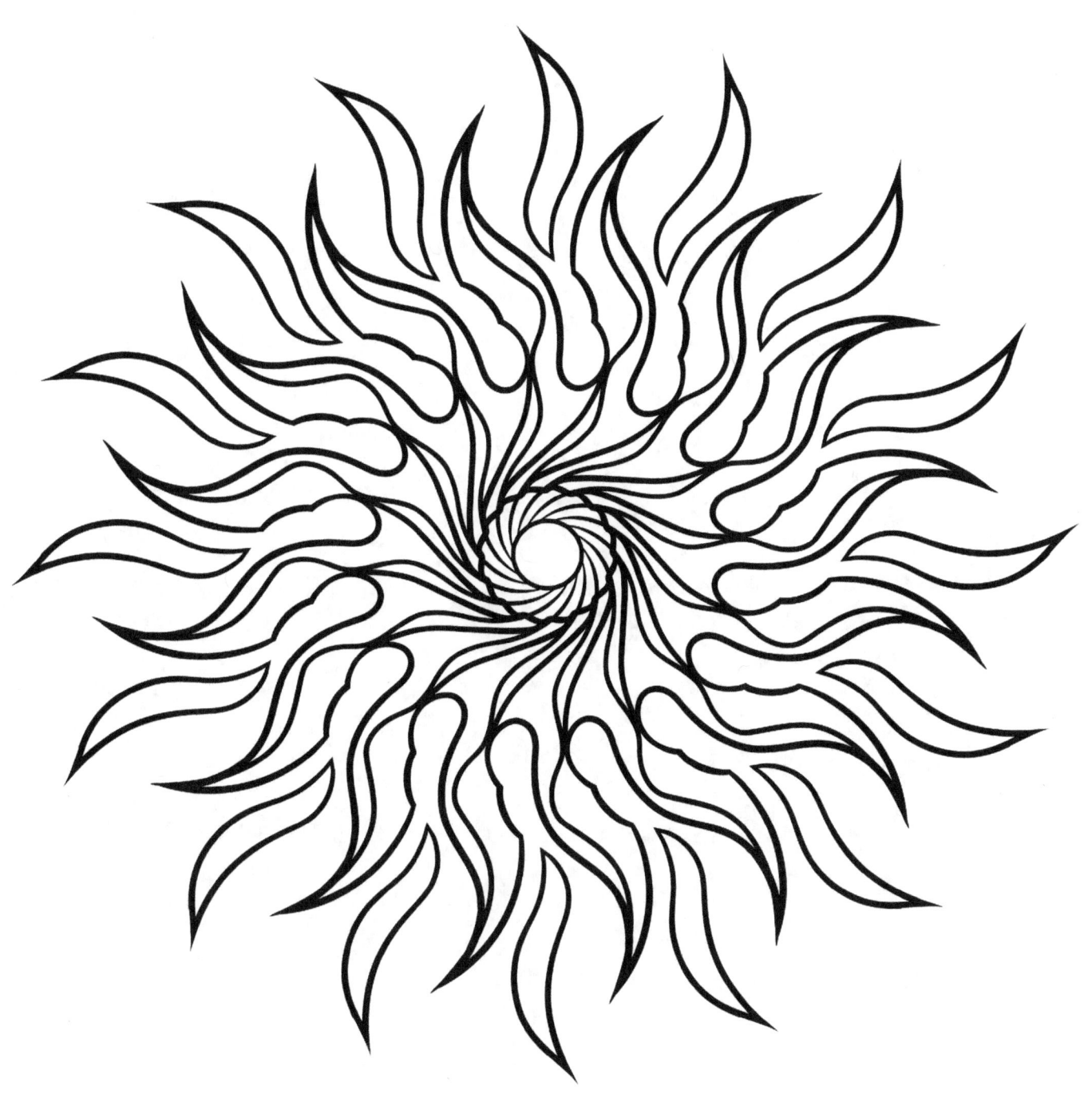

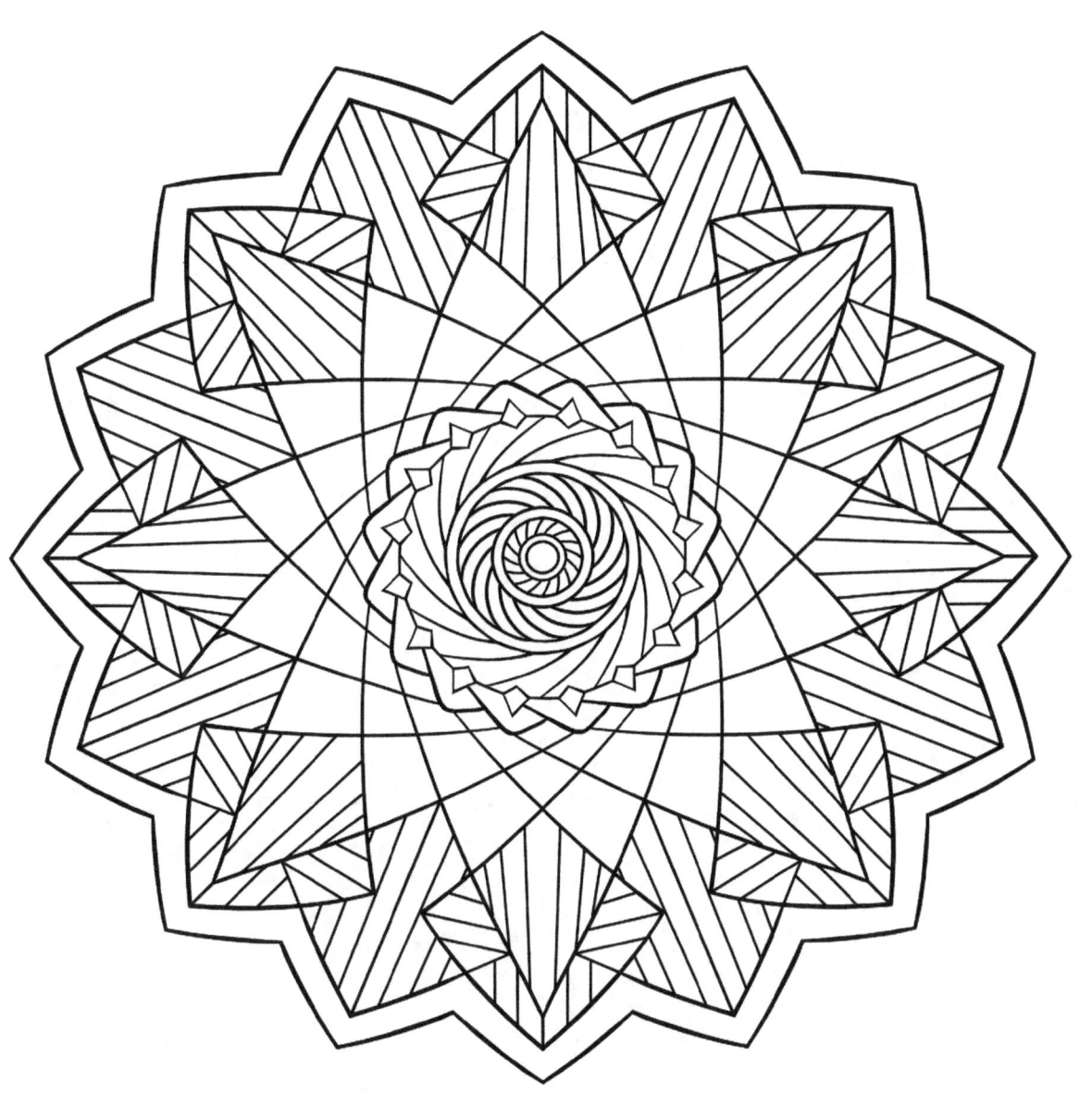

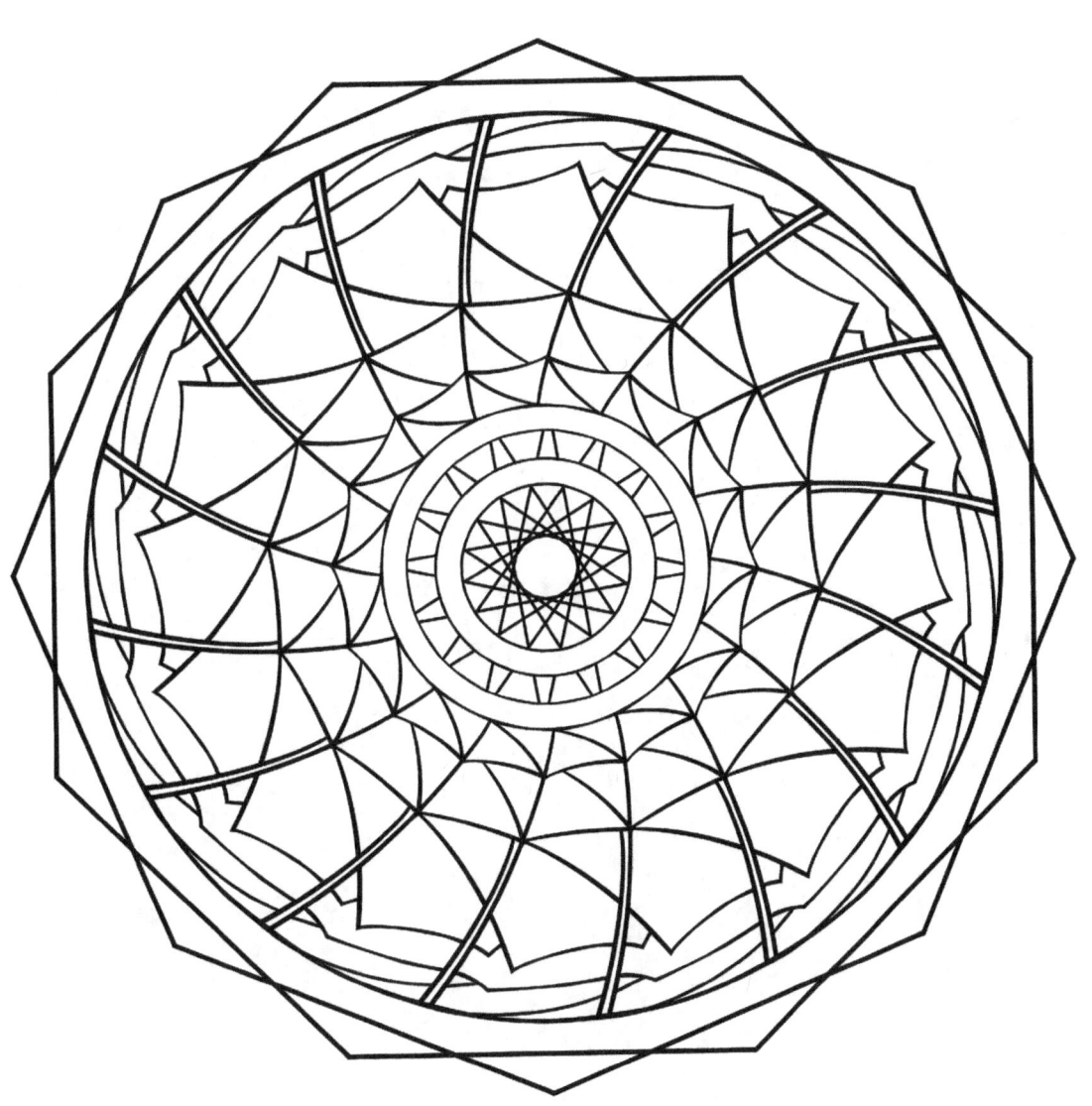

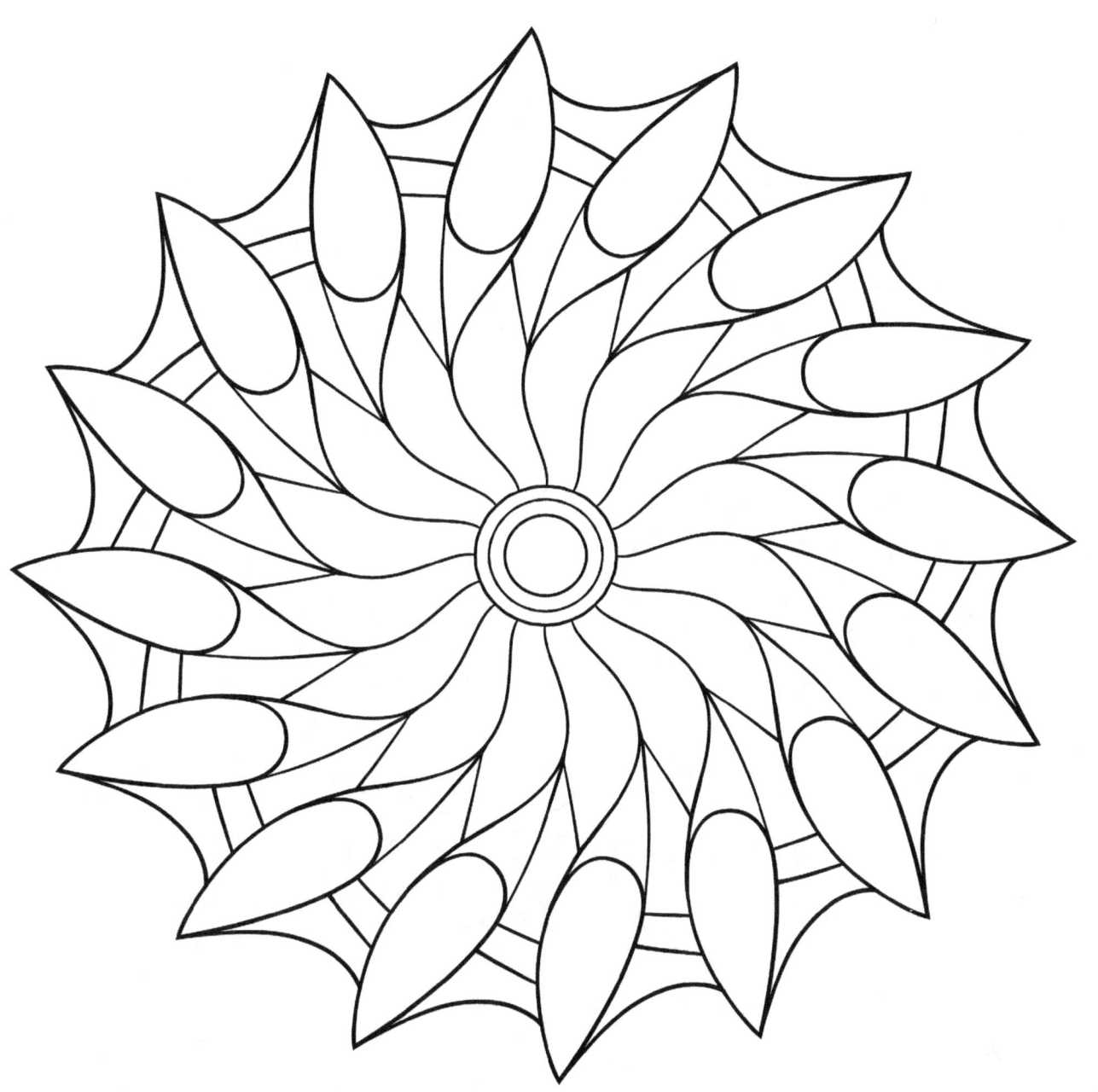

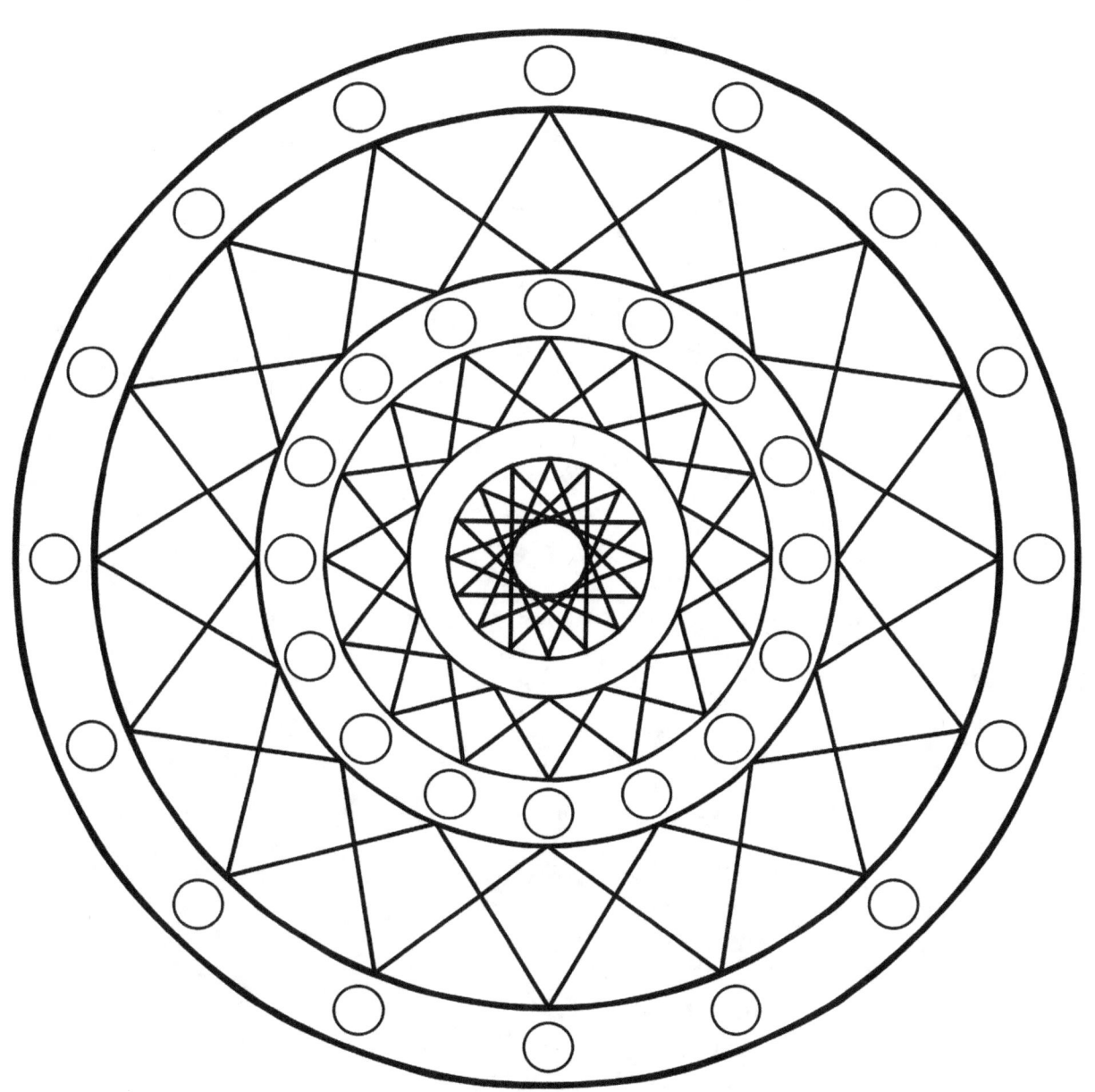

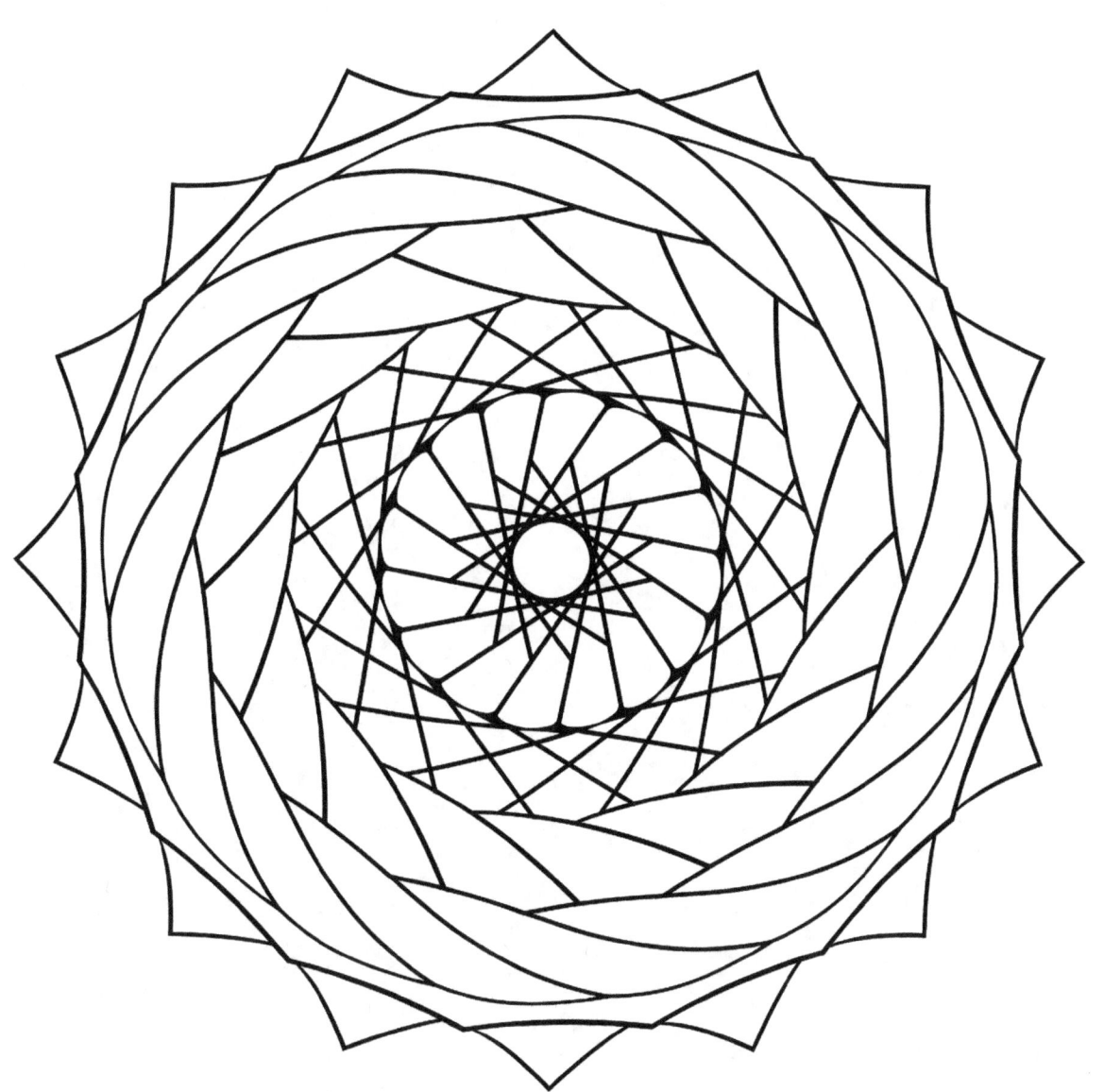

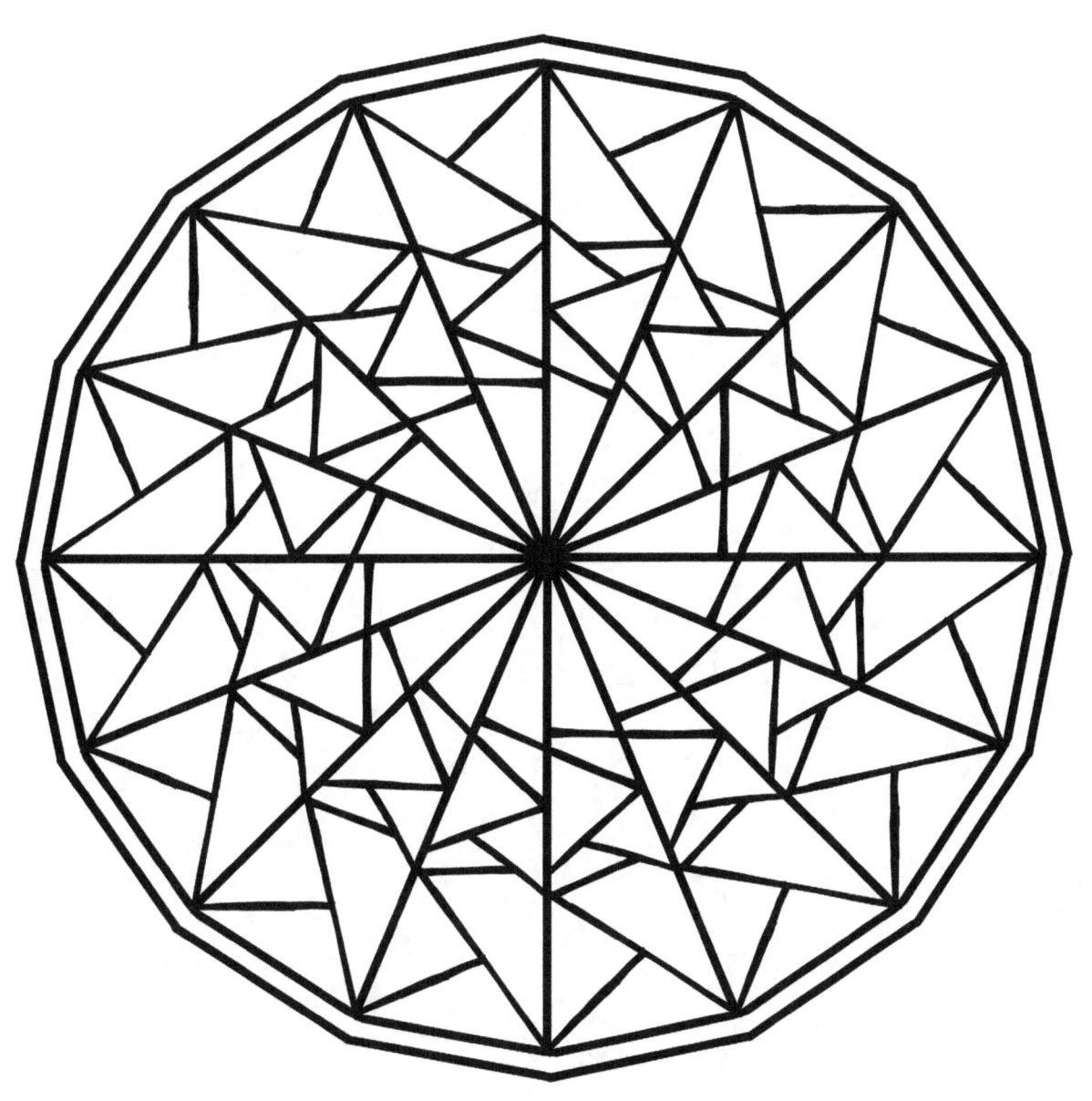

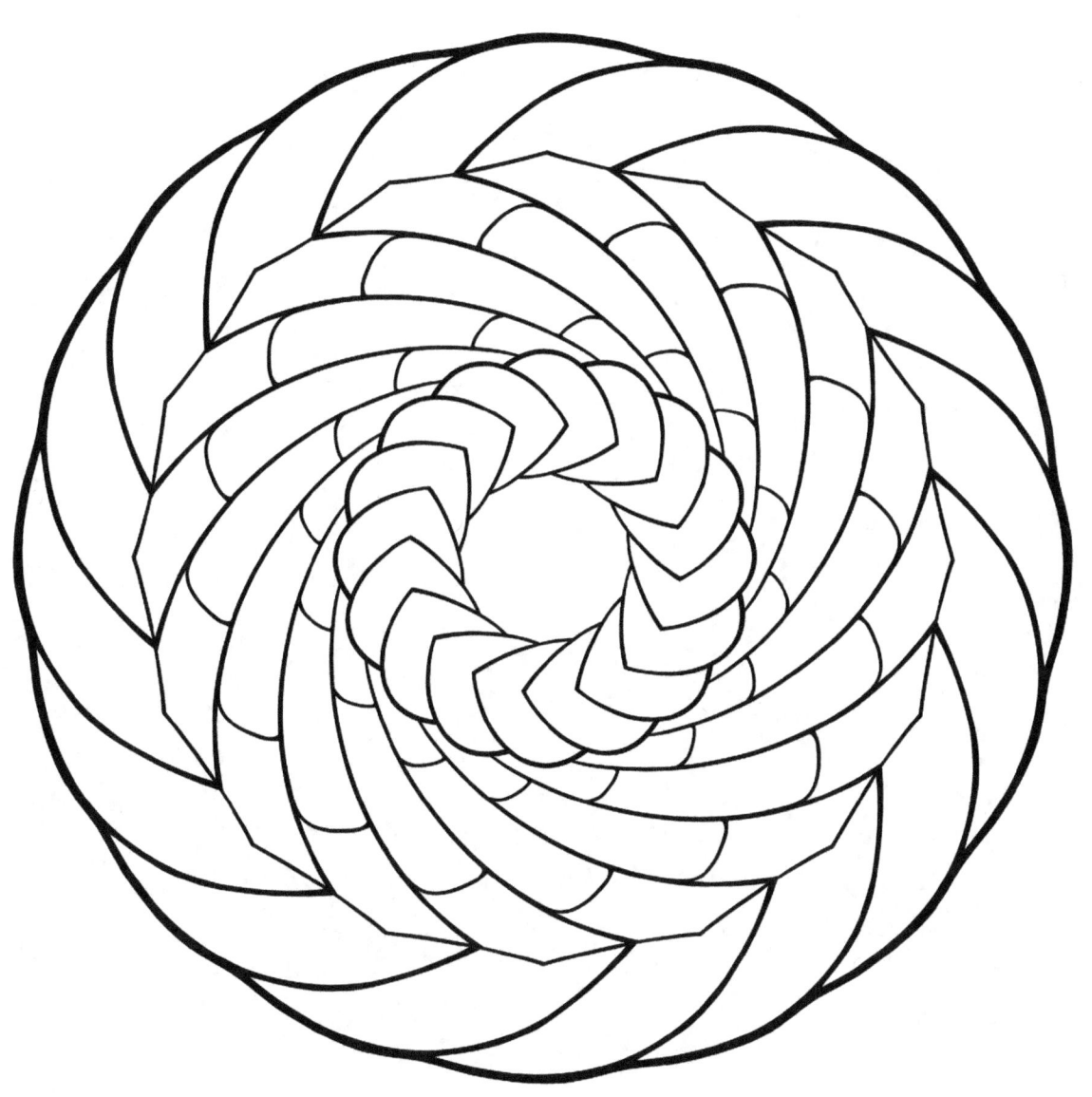

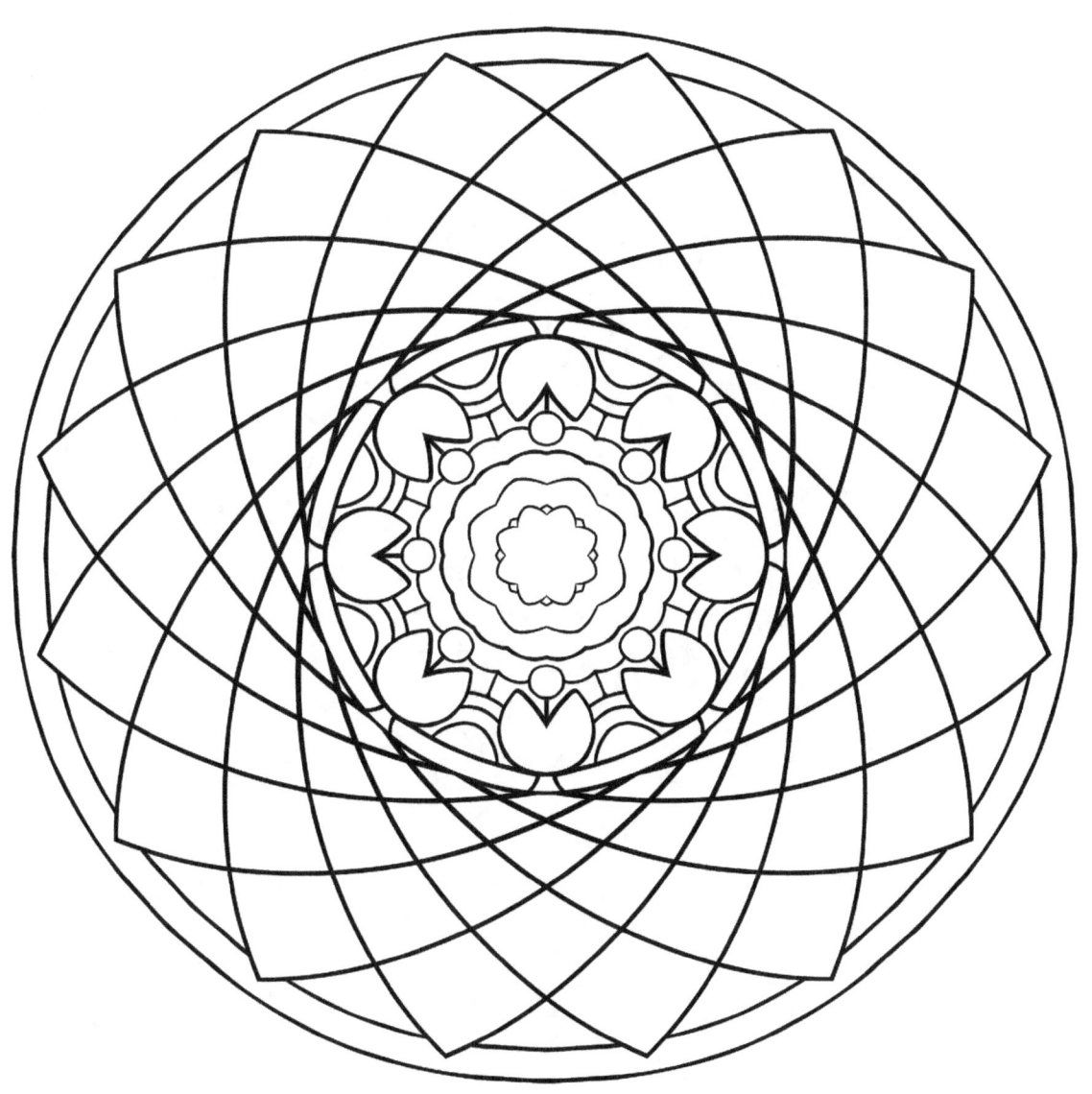

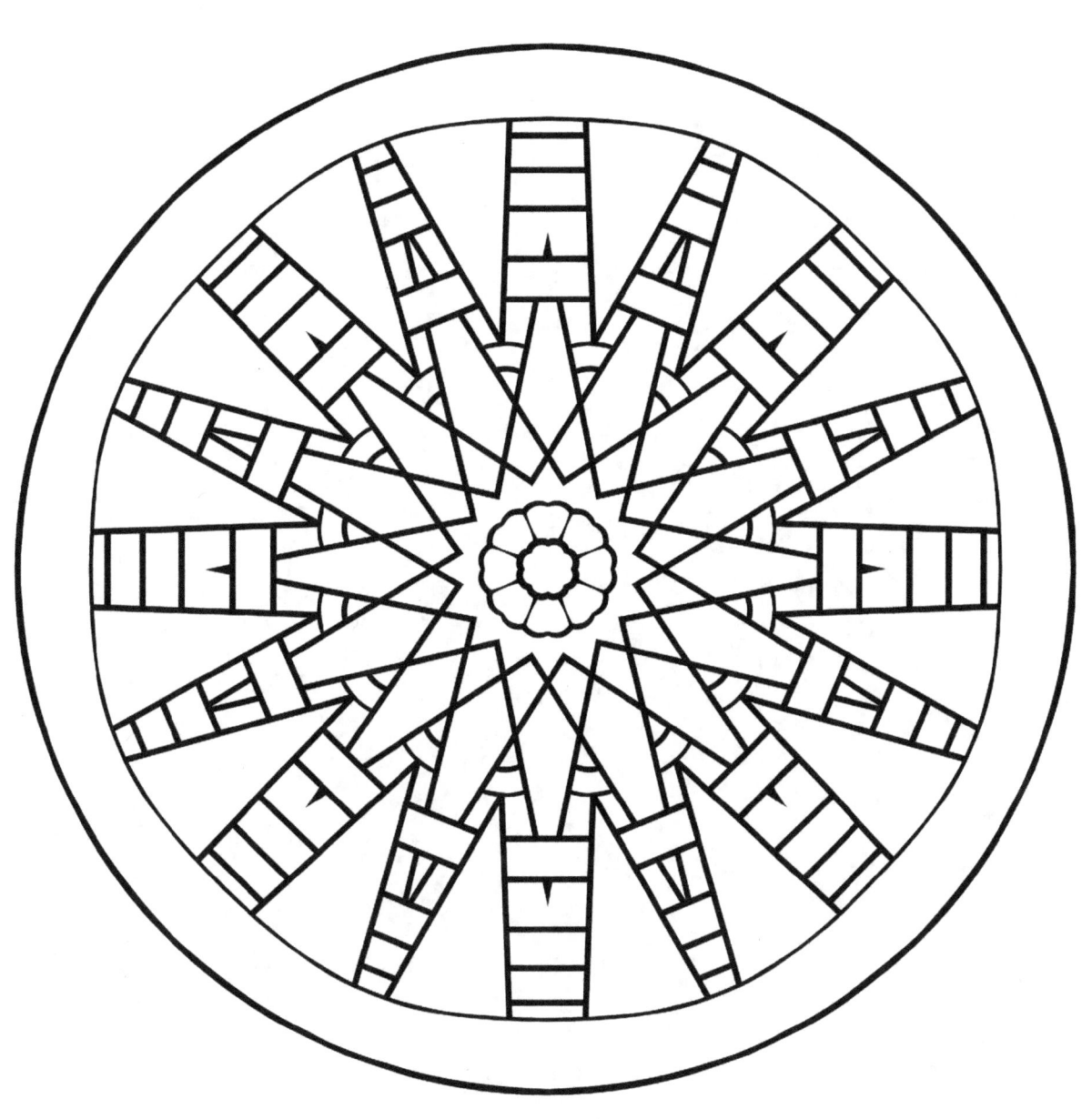

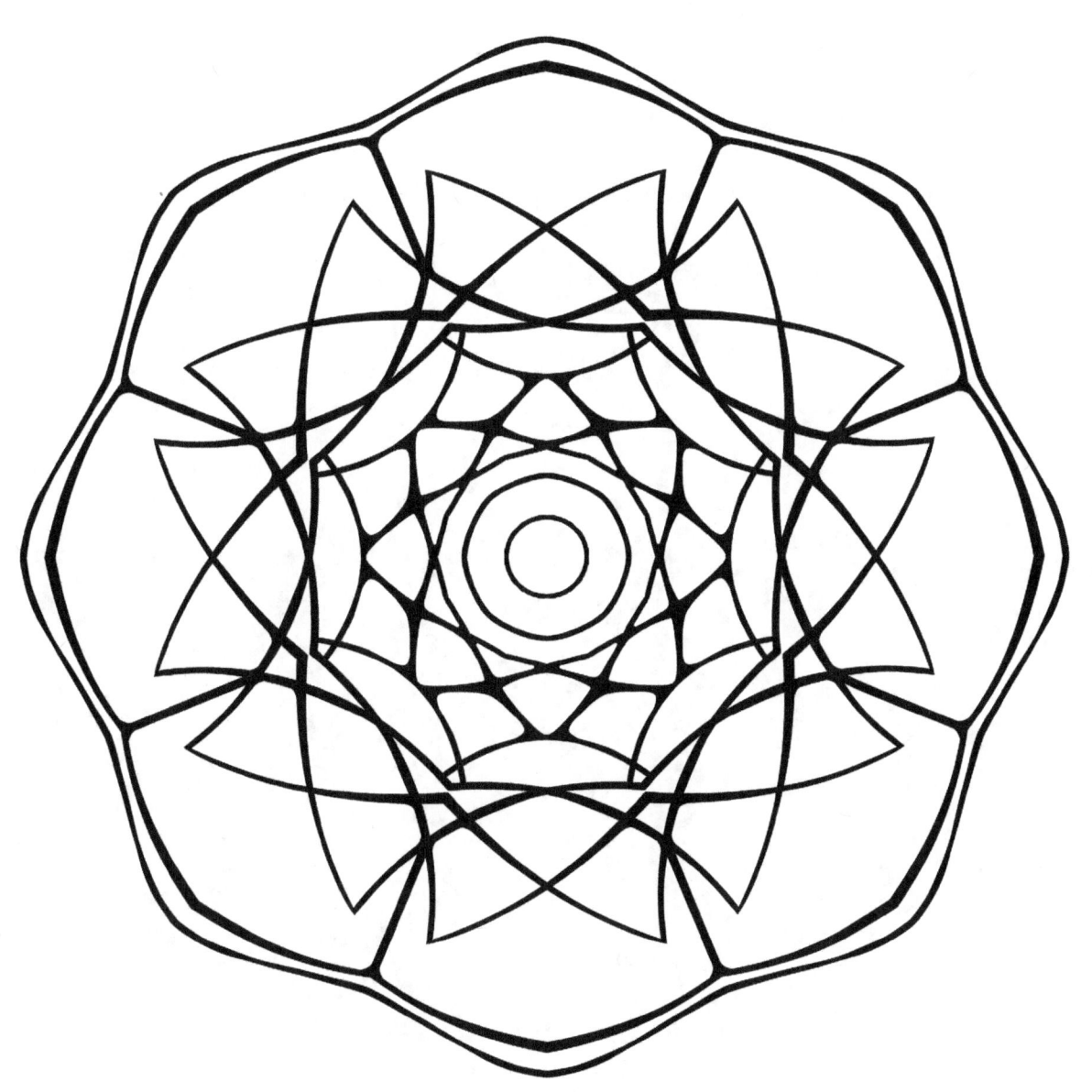

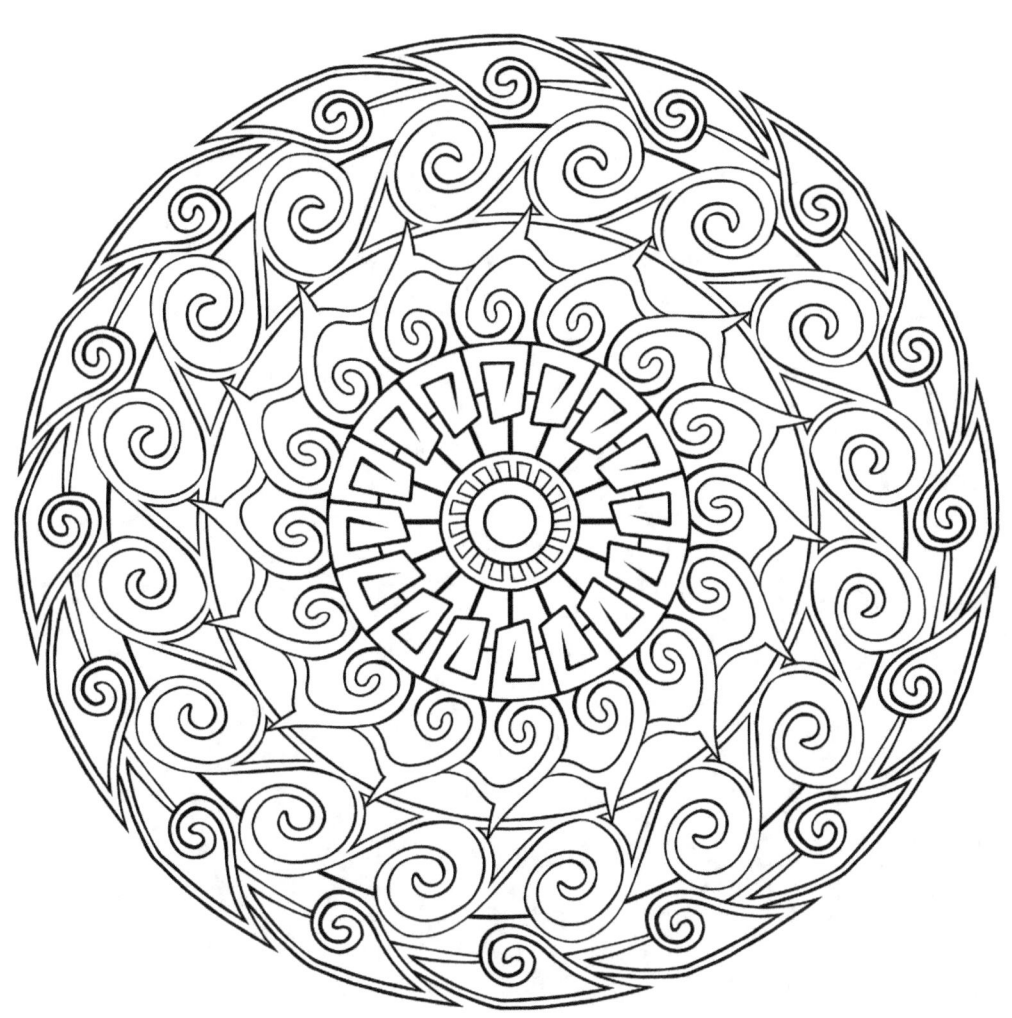

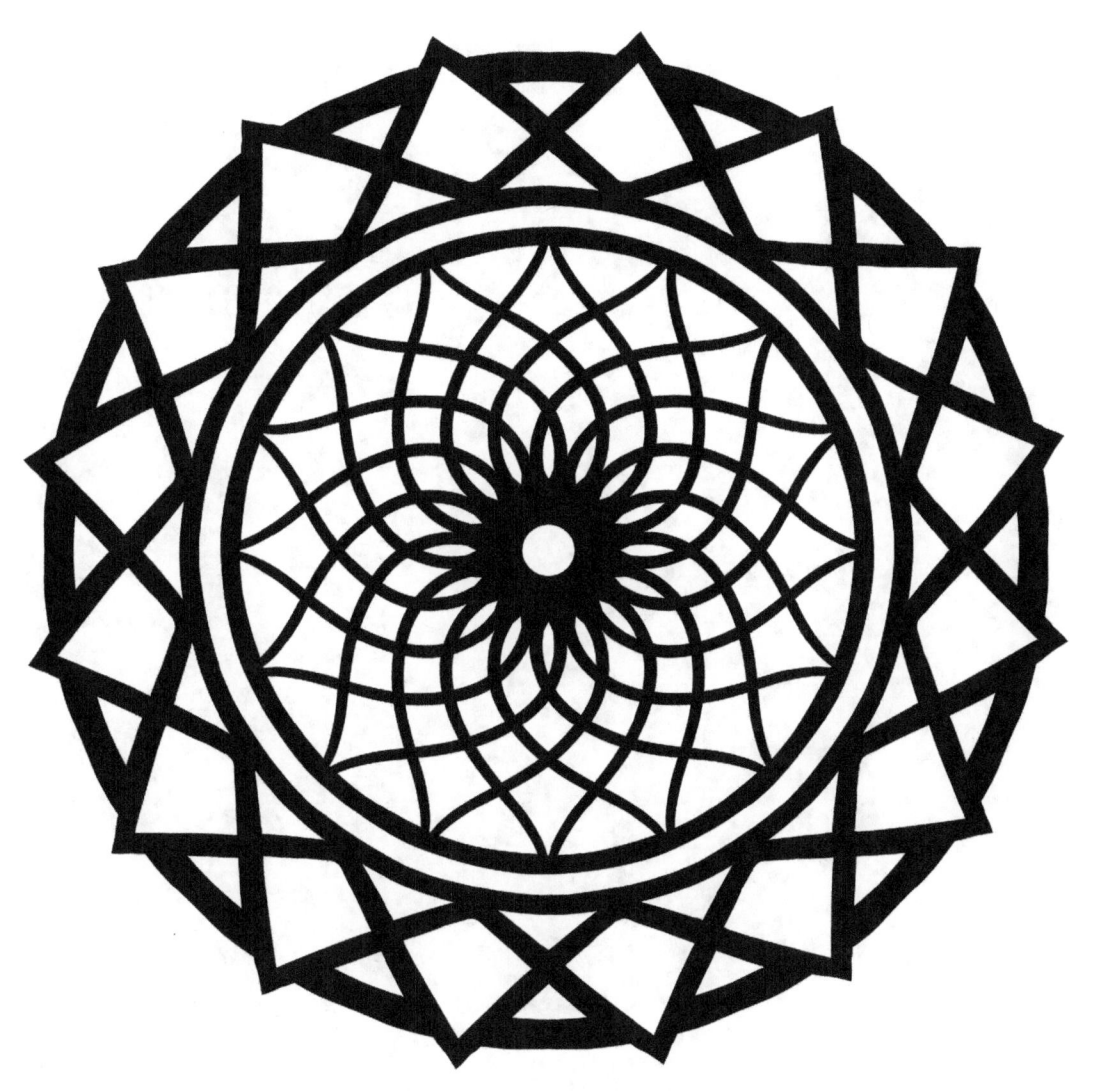

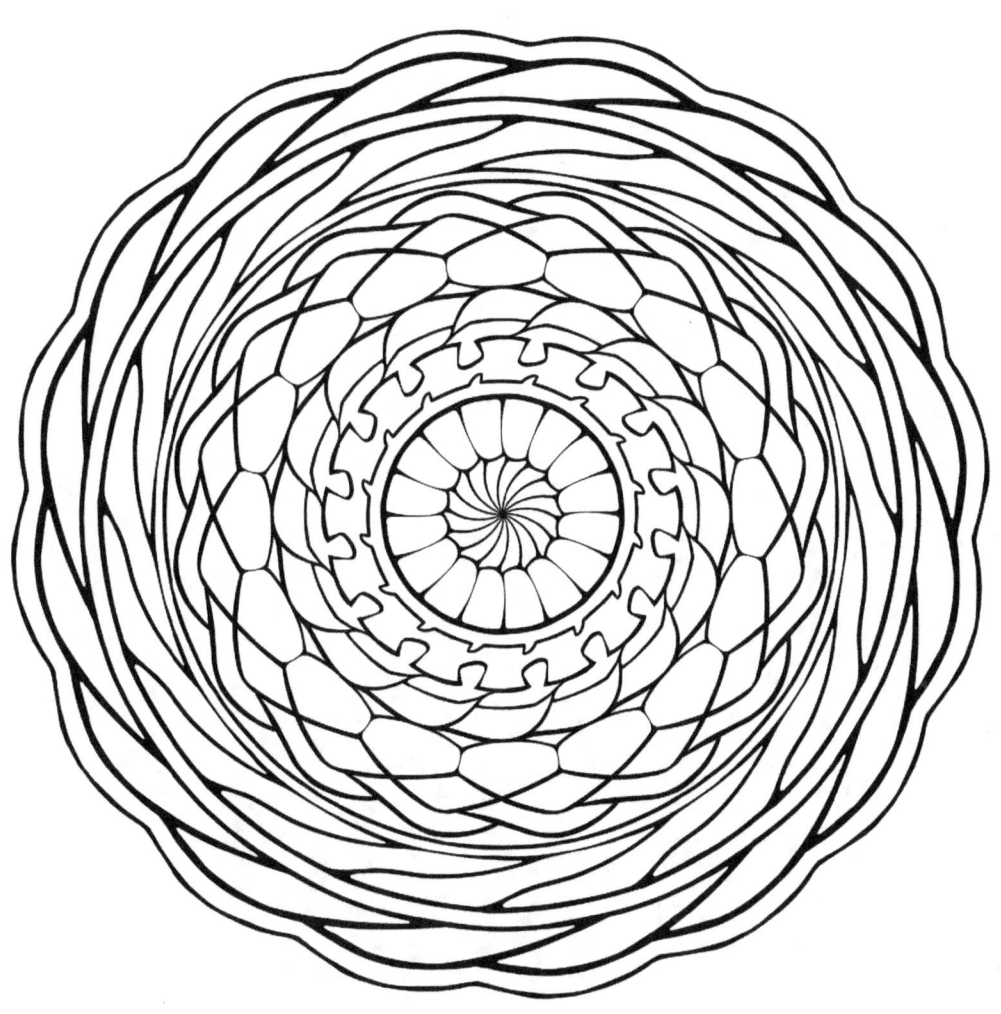

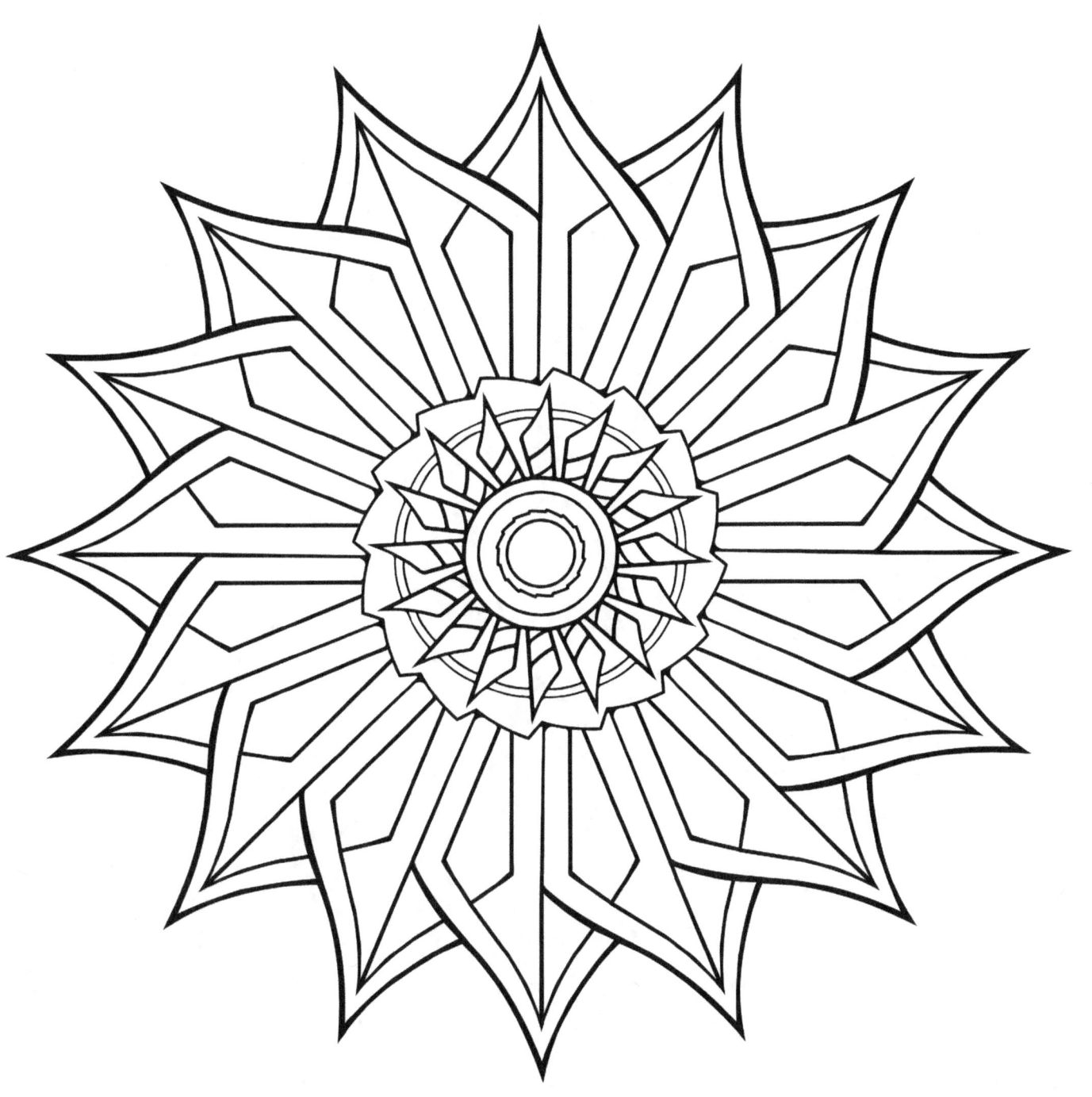

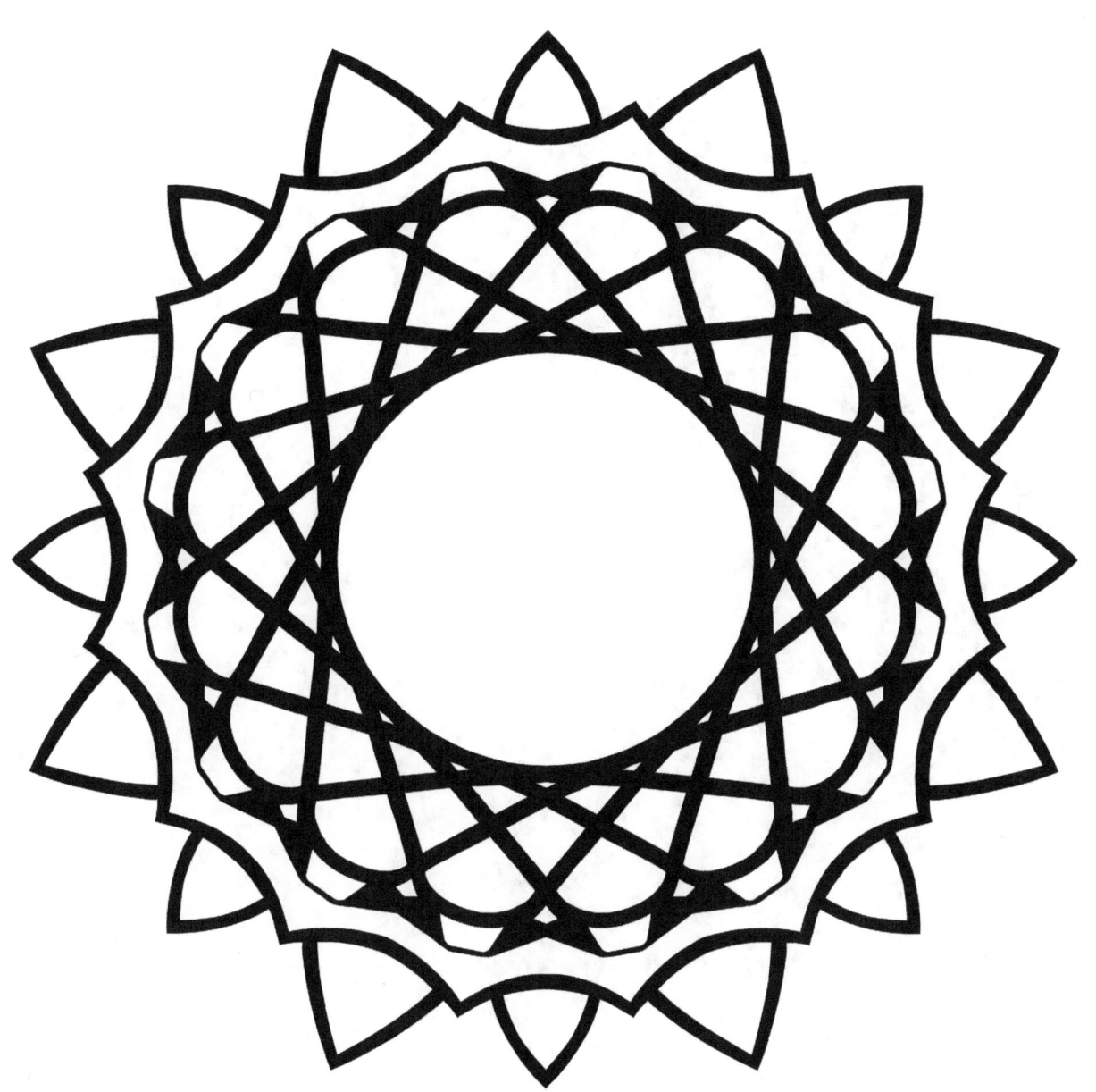

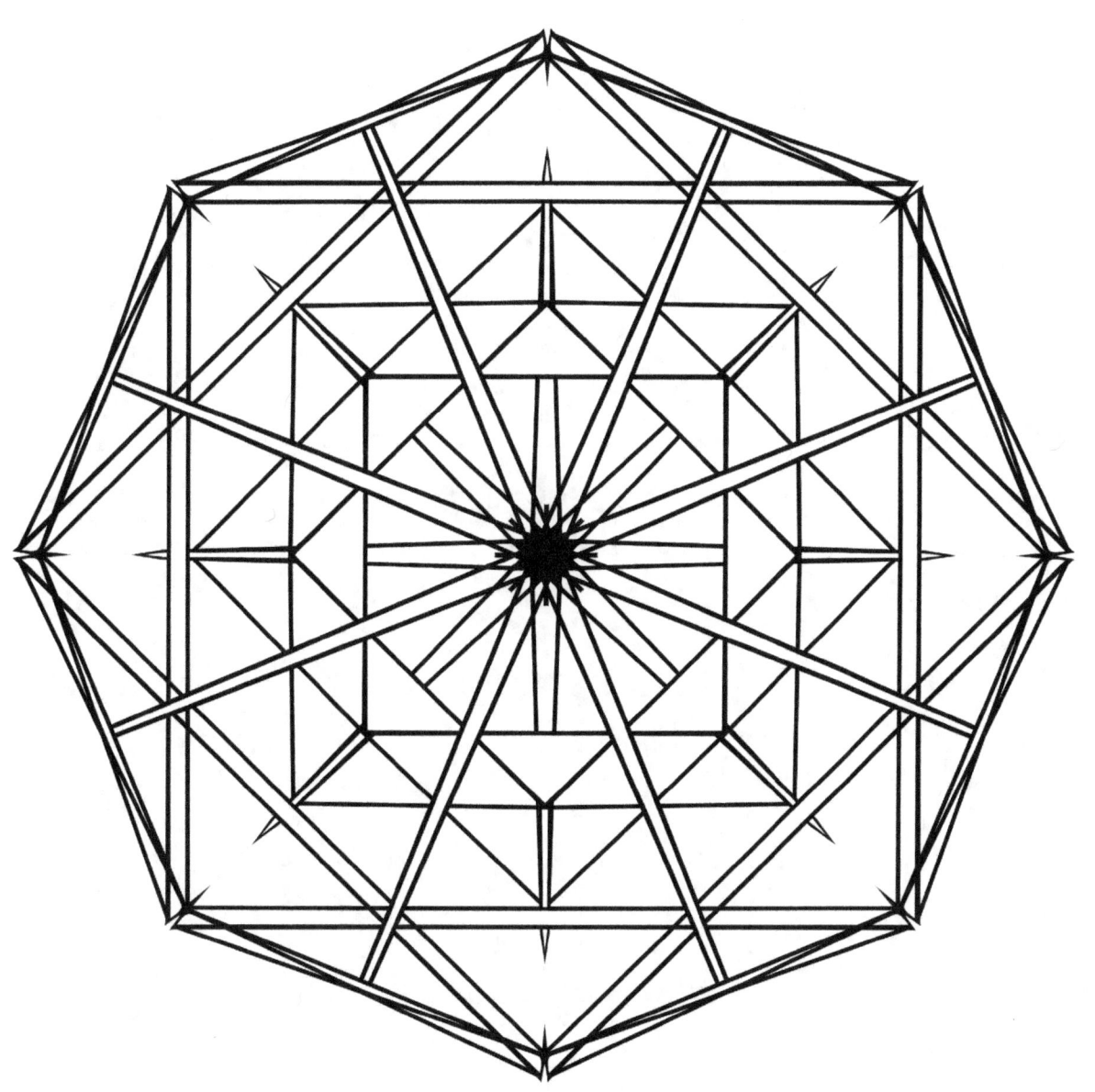

Thank you so much for purchasing my coloring book. Your support means the world to me and fuels my passion for creating more artistic and enjoyable content. I truly hope this book brings you as much joy and relaxation as it did for me while creating it.

Happy Coloring!

-Alter

www.ingramcontent.com/pod-product-compliance
Lightning Source LLC
Chambersburg PA
CBHW062200220526
45470CB00009B/2879